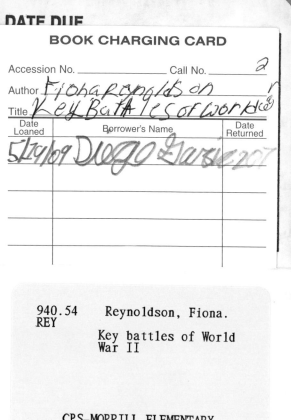

DATE DUE

BOOK CHARGING CARD

Accession No. _____ Call No. _____ 2

Author *Fiona Reynoldson*

Title *Key Battles of World War II*

Date Loaned	Borrower's Name	Date Returned
5/14/09	*Diego Garcia 207*	

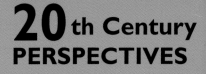
20th Century
PERSPECTIVES

Key Battles of World War II

Fiona Reynoldson

Heinemann Library
Chicago, Illinois

Designed by AMR
Illustrated by Art Construction
Originated by Dot Gradations
Printed in Hong Kong by Wing King Tong

05 04 03 02 01
10 9 8 7 6 5 4 3 2 1

Library of Congress Cataloging-in Publication Data
Reynoldson, Fiona.
    Key battles of World War II / Fiona Reynoldson.
        p. cm. -- (20th-century perspectives)
    Includes bibliographical references and index.
    ISBN 1-57572-438-3
    1. World War, 1939-1945--Campaigns--Juvenile literature. 2. Battles--Juvenile
literature. [1. World War, 1939-1945--Campaigns.] I. Title. II. Series.

D743 .R43 2001
940.54'1--dc21
                                                    00-063455

Acknowledgments
The publishers would like to thank the following for permission to reproduce photographs:
AKG, p.27; Camera press, p.40, 41; Corbis, pp.17, 37, 38; e.t. archive, p.6; Hulton Getty, pp. 8, 12, 20, 42; Imperial War Museum, pp. 9,15; IWM/Camera press, pp.13, 19, 33, 35, 36; IWR/TRH pictures, p.23; IWR/Camera Press, p. 10; Novosti, pp.28, 29, 31; TRH Pictures, pp.5, 18, 22, 25, 26, 30, 39; TRH Pictures/Australian War Memorial, p. 43; TRH/IWM, p. 34.

Cover photograph reproduced with permission of Corbis.

Our thanks to Mark Adamic, Christopher Gibb, Alastair Gray, and Lorna Gray for their help.

Every effort has been made to contact copyright holders of any material reproduced in this book. Any omissions will be rectified in subsequent printings if notice is given to the publishers.

Some words are shown in bold, **like this.** You can find out what they mean by looking in the glossary.

Contents

The Invasion of Poland, September 1939

By the summer of 1939, most people in Europe knew that war was unavoidable. German leader Adolf Hitler had demanded or taken more and more land around Germany. Britain and France had vowed to stand firm. If Hitler turned to attack Poland, they would declare war.

The Poles were expecting an attack. They had soldiers stationed along the frontier. But when the invasion came, it was so fast and so furious that it was over in weeks. It was the shortest and most decisive of all the German campaigns in World War II. The German plan was straightforward. Several armies would attack Poland in a pincer movement, closing at Warsaw, the Polish capital, then they would destroy the encircled Polish armies.

Poland, for its part, intended to hold the invaders long enough for the British and French to send soldiers to help. This proved to be impossible. Polish reserve soldiers were being called to join their army units as the first German **panzers** rolled over the frontiers. At 4:45 A.M. on September 1, 1939, two German army groups moved as planned with nearly 2,000 tanks, and in the air 2,000 planes launched a massive air strike on all bases in Poland, including Warsaw. Most of the Polish Air Force was destroyed within two days; though it had damaged or destroyed about 500 German planes. Within a matter of hours, Poland's small navy was overcome. Three **destroyers** and two submarines managed to slip away and escape to Britain.

Despite poor Polish roads, the Germans advanced up to 16 mi (25 km) on the first day.

This map shows Northern and Central Europe in September 1939. On September 1, Germany invaded Poland from the west and north. On September 17, the Soviet Union invaded from the east. Poland was defeated within two weeks and divided between Germany and the Soviet Union.

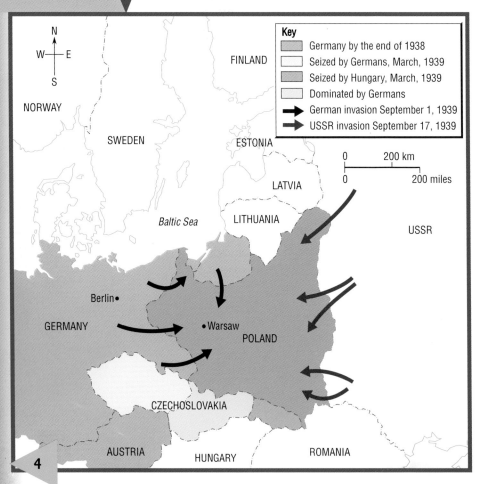

Key
- Germany by the end of 1938
- Seized by Germans, March, 1939
- Seized by Hungary, March, 1939
- Dominated by Germans
- → German invasion September 1, 1939
- → USSR invasion September 17, 1939

FINLAND
NORWAY
SWEDEN
ESTONIA
LATVIA
Baltic Sea
LITHUANIA
USSR
Berlin
GERMANY
Warsaw
POLAND
CZECHOSLOVAKIA
AUSTRIA
HUNGARY
ROMANIA

0   200 km
0   200 miles

By September 7, they were within 40 miles (65 km) of Warsaw. The Polish government had left the city the day before. As the Germans advanced, the Russians saw their opportunity and invaded Poland from the east. To the surprise and dismay of Britain and France, **fascist** Germany had made a treaty with **communist** Russia in August 1939. The two nations were supposed to be hated rivals. One of the secret clauses of the **treaty** was that they would carve up Poland between them. However, the Russians too were surprised by the German's speedy advance and did not want Germany to take over all of Poland.

These Stuka dive-bombers were part of Germany's "lightning war," or Blitzkrieg, attack on Poland in September 1939.

Blitzkrieg–lightning war

The invasion of Poland was the first example of the German **Blitzkrieg**, or "lightning war." Blitzkrieg made use of fast-moving tanks and armored vehicles, supported by aircraft. These forces could penetrate quickly and deep behind enemy defenses, and then circle around and destroy the enemy army. Poland and the rest of the world were taken by surprise. This would happen again and again in the early days of the war. It was at this point that Britain and France declared war on Germany. This spread the fighting across Western Europe and set the scene for the rest of the war.

WHAT HAPPENED TO THE POLISH ARMY	
TAKEN PRISONER BY GERMANS	ABOUT 600,000
ESCAPED, MANY TO FIGHT WITH **ALLIES**	100,000

How Had the War Come About?

World War I ended in 1918. It was called the war to end all wars. More than seven million men had died. Most people never wanted to fight another war. The victorious **Allies** decided to create the League of Nations. Over 50 countries joined it, but the United States did not. In theory, if one country was attacked, all the others would band together and refuse to trade with the attacker. This would mean there would be no more wars. However, if countries really wanted to fight, they did so. The League of Nations was like a lion with no teeth.

The Nazis were excellent at **propaganda.** This 1923 election poster reads: "Workers of the brow and of the fist, vote for Hitler, the frontline soldier."

Peace or armistice?

"This is not a peace treaty, it is an armistice [cease-fire] for twenty years."

The Allied commander-in-chief, Marshal Foch's comment on the terms of the Treaty of Versailles, 1919.

The aftermath of World War I

After World War I, Germany was devastated. According to the **Treaty of Versailles**, the victorious Allies made sure that Germany lost land, that it could only have a small army and no navy or air force, and that it paid large sums of money for damage done during the war.

The rise of Hitler and the Nazis

The large sums of money that Germany had to pay for the war damage were called **reparations**. France was particularly eager to receive reparations because so much of northern France had been destroyed by four years of war. Germany hated the reparations. Many Germans thought they symbolized that their country was given all the blame for starting World War I. They also felt that they should never have lost the war and that somehow they were betrayed into surrender. When the future German leader Adolf Hitler appeared on the scene in the 1920s, he promised to make Germany rich and great again. He joined and then took over the Nationalist Socialist German Workers Party, which became known as the Nazi Party.

The Wall Street Crash and worldwide depression

The U.S. **stock market's** crash on Wall Street in 1929 affected countries all over the world and led to widespread unemployment. It became known as the Great Depression. In Germany, Hitler said he would create jobs and he would make businesses work. In 1933, he was elected **chancellor**, and shortly afterward began to call himself "*Führer*," or leader, of Germany.

The road to war

After 1933, there were more jobs in Germany. However, there were more jobs in other countries, too. The world had begun to pull out of the worst of the depression, though Hitler took the credit for saving Germany. At the same time, he was determined to avenge Germany's defeat in World War I. He started to build an army again and to demand German land back.

Here, British Prime Minister Neville Chamberlain is shown returning from Germany in September 1938. He had just concluded the Munich Agreement, which he claimed would bring "peace for our time." Within a year Britain and Germany were at war.

Other countries were nervous about this but no one wanted another war. Britain felt that Germany should be treated better. In 1936, when German soldiers marched into the Ruhr—an important industrial area—and took it back from France, no one really protested. This was followed by the German invasion of Austria in 1938 and the demand for part of **Czechoslovakia**. The British and French agreed because nearly all the people in that part of Czechoslovakia were German. This agreement was signed in Munich. The policy of saying "yes" to Hitler's demands was called **appeasement**.

Within months, Hitler wanted more of Czechoslovakia. It was obvious that war was coming. Hitler had stated that he wanted more **Lebensraum,** or "living space," for the German people in the east, and he was not going to stop unless he was forced. On September 1, 1939, after protecting his interests with a **treaty** with Russia, Germany invaded Poland in the lightning attack, or **Blitzkrieg.**

Blitzkrieg Goes West, May 1940

After the invasion of Poland in September 1939, very little happened for months. This became known as the "phony war." Then in April 1940, Germany invaded Denmark and Norway and followed this by invading the Netherlands and Belgium, which was neutral.

The German attack

The German attack began on May 10, and the Netherlands was overwhelmed in a few days while the main German army moved on to Belgium. The Belgians fought bravely but the Germans were already attacking from the north through the now conquered Netherlands as well as from the east. **Paratroopers** were dropped at key points, and at rivers a combination of **dive bombers** and armored vehicles often panicked the soldiers defending the crossings. At the fortress of Eben Emael, German **glider troops** landed on the roof and blasted their way inside, forcing the Belgian soldiers to surrender. French and British soldiers committed to help the Belgians fell back before the German attack.

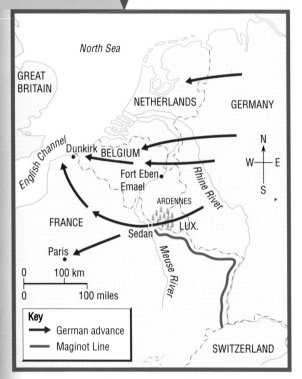

The German advance in May 1940 forced British and French troops back to Dunkirk.

Why were the Germans so successful?

The Germans had about the same number of soldiers and tanks as the **Allies,** which included the French, British, Belgians, and Dutch, though they had more airplanes. However, the Allies were a mixture of nationalities and abilities, and they were facing a very well-organized army and air force whose leaders had planned and practiced this attack which became known as Operation Sicklestroke. The German tanks were organized into ten **panzer** divisions and worked closely with the air force, as they had done in Poland. The Germans had a very clear idea of what they wanted to do while the Allies were simply defending. Added to this, the ordinary soldier did not want to fight. Germany was fired up for war while the Allies were not.

The fall of France

By mid-May, the Germans were bursting through the hilly forests of the Ardennes and into France. The French had always assumed that tanks and other vehicles could not get through the Ardennes so they had left it almost undefended. Instead, after World War I, they had spent eight years building the vast **Maginot Line** to the south to stop Germany from ever being able to invade. The mobile German army just went around it.

The retreat to Britain

On May 28, the Belgians finally surrendered, by which time the British and many of the French had been forced back to Dunkirk, on the English Channel, where they were encircled by the Germans. However, Hitler halted his army so that they could regroup before their final victory. This gave the British a two-day breathing space. On May 27, the British Royal Navy started to **evacuate** soldiers from the Dunkirk beaches.

This painting by war artist Charles Chundall shows the dramatic rescue of Allied troops from Dunkirk. Smaller boats ferry soldiers out to the waiting troop ships, while the German army bombs the beaches.

Thousands and thousands of Allied soldiers lined the beaches. The big ships often had to stand well off shore while smaller boats ferried the soldiers from the beaches. Everything was left behind except the clothes the soldiers wore and their rifles. Sometimes even their coats were left in the sea as they waded out to the boats. The German air force bombed the beaches but most of the bombs plunged into the soft sand and did little harm. By June 4, the evacuation stopped. The Germans broke through but 338,226 men had been rescued, a third of them French. The British army had lost all its tanks, guns, and trucks, but at least it lived to fight another day.

No one knew how soon that day might be. In fact, Hitler intended to follow up the defeat of France with the invasion of Britain. The key battle would be the Battle of Britain.

Operation Dynamo

Operation Dynamo was the code name for the Dunkirk evacuation. It was hoped that the navy could rescue 35,000 soldiers. In the event, the rescue lasted nine days and brought ten times that number of men back to England. The government ordered that any boats in southern England over 98 feet (30 m) long had to take part. Naval officers were put in charge, but civilian crews endangered their own lives by making many trips to help with the evacuation.

The Battle of Britain, July to September 1940

In July 1940, Hitler gave orders for the preparation of a seaborne invasion of Britain, called Operation Sealion. However, first he had to destroy the Royal Air Force (RAF) so that it could not bomb the German invasion ships as they sailed for Britain.

On July 10, the German air force, or **Luftwaffe,** made their first attack on British ships in the English Channel. However, Britain used their new **radar** equipment to detect the bombers and sent four squadrons of British fighters to drive them off. This was the beginning of the Battle of Britain.

A long hot summer

It was a beautiful summer. Day after day the clear blue skies over the coast and countryside of southeast England were the scene of desperate battles between German and British planes. The German bombers headed for RAF airfields. The slow, heavy bombers were escorted by fighter planes such as the very fast Messerschmitt 109. The RAF fighter planes were mainly Hurricanes and Spitfires. They were not as fast as the Messerschmitts but they were able to turn more quickly. This was important in the twisting and turning dogfights in the skies.

Other things helped in the battle, too. Air Chief Marshal Dowding was head of RAF Fighter Command. He made use of the new invention of radar. The radar stations picked up German bombers on their screens as

This photograph shows RAF pilots scrambling to their planes during the Battle of Britain in the summer of 1940. At the height of the battle, pilots were making as many as seven **sorties** *a day.*

they were flying over the English Channel. In addition, the Observer Corps consisted of people on duty watching for German planes all along the south part of Britain. By using new land-to-air radio, which the Germans did not have, RAF fighter planes were told where the German bombers were.

On August 15, the Germans made their biggest attack of the battle so far. Fighting went on all day. By now, the British were becoming anxious about the low supply of pilots and fighter planes. Pilots were flying up to seven sorties a day and sleeping when they could. Then, on September 7, the Germans switched to bombing London.

The final battle

On September 15, a desperate battle took place over London. The *Luftwaffe* flew in vast numbers. The RAF were forced to use all of their planes. The fighting continued all day. At the end of the day, the Germans lost more planes than the British. The Battle of Britain was over. From then on, the Germans switched their attack to bombing British cities.

The bombing of London gave the RAF a much-needed break from the costly attacks on its airfields and time for them to rebuild their weakened forces.

The Battle of Britain marked the limits of German expansion in the West and showed the world that the German forces could be stopped.

Frank Webster was a Spitfire fighter pilot in the Battle of Britain, flying with 610 Squadron. He was shot down and killed on August 26, 1940. Frank is wearing a flying suit and fur-lined boots. Fighter pilots often cut off the fur collar so they could turn their heads easily and spot enemy planes approaching.

WHO FOUGHT IN THE BATTLE OF BRITAIN?
NATIONALITIES OF PILOTS FLYING WITH THE RAF IN THE BATTLE OF BRITAIN

UNITED KINGDOM	2,429
POLISH	141
NEW ZEALAND	102
CANADIAN	90
CZECHOSLOVAK	86
BELGIAN	29
AUSTRALIAN	21
SOUTH AFRICAN	21
FRENCH	13
AMERICAN	7
RHODESIAN	2
OTHERS	11
RAF PILOTS KILLED	510

The Battle of the Atlantic, 1940–1943

If Britain was going to hold out against the Germans, it would need guns, airplanes, ships, tanks, oil, and food. All these were in short supply in 1940. At this time, Britain only produced one third of the food it needed to feed its population. The rest came from other countries by sea. The desperate struggle to bring food and other goods to Britain cost thousands of lives and ships, as Germany tried to cut off essential supplies. The main supply route was across the Atlantic Ocean from the United States. At first, German submarines, called **U-boats,** attacked the merchant ships as they were approaching Britain from the west. However, by 1940, this area was well patrolled by the British and the U-boats moved further out into the Atlantic Ocean.

The Atlantic Gap

The major problem facing the **Allies** in protecting the merchant ships from German attack was that vast stretches of the Atlantic could not be patrolled by air. At this time, planes could only fly about 186 miles (300 km) before they had to return to base to be refueled. This left the merchant ships unprotected for a large part of the ocean, known as the Atlantic Gap. The Allies did not have enough escort vessels. Until early 1941, the U-boats were very successful.

This U.S. Navy flying boat is watching over a convoy of supply ships in the North Atlantic in November 1941. These planes played an important role in keeping the sea routes open.

Allied convoys

Many of the German submarines were based on the west coast of France. From there, groups of U-boats called "wolf packs" went out to hunt the Allied **convoys**. A typical convoy consisted of 40 to 50 merchant ships sailing in columns to form a box shape. A small number of escort ships patrolled the edges of the convoy. In conditions ranging from sunny, calm weather with a gentle swell to violent, gale-force winds with waves yards (meters) high, the convoy would move slowly towards Britain from America.

German submarine wolf packs

The wolf packs often waited, half submerged, ahead of the convoy, ready to attack. The escort ships could only detect submarines for about one mile (one km) using Asdic, a device using sound waves underwater.

With few escort ships, it was easy for U-boats to sneak through and attack a convoy, so that in 1941, one in four ships sailing to Britain was sunk.

However, once one of the submarines launched its torpedoes, the naval escort ships set out to hunt the submarine. Apart from Asdic, they used **radar** to detect any submarines on the surface and listening devices to "hear" the submarine engines and propellers beneath the surface. Once detected, the escort ship used underwater bombs called depth charges thrown out from the back of the ship. These were set to explode at different depths and often in patterns to cover the area in which the submarine was probably lurking.

As the Battle of the Atlantic progressed, the Allies totaled the monthly tonnage of merchant ships and their cargoes that had been sunk against the number of submarines sunk. The Germans did similar calculations. From 1943, the trend began to go against the Germans, with more and more submarines sunk. This turning point was brought about by the larger numbers of escort ships covering each convoy, the increasing range of aircraft, and the introduction of small aircraft carriers from which planes could fly. All this closed the Atlantic Gap and made it increasingly difficult for the German submarines to go undetected.

These sailors are crewman aboard a German U-boat.

Bringing troops

Men as well as goods had to be brought across the Atlantic to fight in Europe. The *Queen Mary* and the *Queen Elizabeth* were two of the biggest passenger liners ever built. In peacetime, they carried about 2,000 passengers and more than 1,000 officers and crew. In wartime, they carried 15,000 soldiers from Canada and the United States on each trip. The liners were so fast that they traveled alone because no U-boat could catch up with them.

A World War

The trading links between Britain and the United States allowed Britain to maintain its fight against Germany from 1940 to 1941.

Meanwhile, there were changes on the opposite side of the world. Japan was emerging as a powerful nation. By 1931, Japan had gained land in northern China. In 1937, it had invaded more of mainland China, capturing all of the important cities and ports. Now the Japanese could ship coal and iron ore from China to Japan to feed the heavy industries needed to make machines, ships, airplanes, and tanks.

The all-out war on China had been watched by many foreign observers. It had led to mounting tension between the United States and Japan. The relations between Japan and Britain weren't any better. Japan aimed to cut China's trade routes to the outside world and this affected Britain. In 1940, the Japanese succeeded in closing the Burma Road that led from southwest China to British-held Burma for a few months. This road was important because it linked the Nationalist Chinese forces with the British Empire.

The tension of fear and of concentration exhausted this American soldier so much that he could not close his jaw or focus his eyes. Later in the war, the U.S. Marines called this "the 2,000 yard stare." It was typical of soldiers fighting in close combat on any side in the war.

The Soviet Union and Japan

Then in 1941, the Japanese signed a nonaggression pact, an agreement that neither country would attack the other, with the Soviet Union. This was very important to Japan, which could not expand in the Pacific if there was any risk of the Soviet Union attacking. It also suited the Soviet Union, which was facing Nazi Germany on its western front and could not afford a conflict with Japan in the east.

The French, the Dutch, the United States, and Japan

In July 1941, Japanese soldiers invaded French **Indo-China** with the aim of taking the Dutch **East Indies**. Both France and the Netherlands had been occupied by the Germans in 1940 and could not defend their **colonies**. The oil-rich Dutch East Indies were particularly important to Japan. The campaign in China was draining Japan's oil reserves. This was extremely serious because 80 percent of Japan's oil came from the United States, which was becoming increasingly unfriendly to Japan.

Breaking off trading relations

The invasion of French Indo-China meant that Japanese bombers and ships were within easy striking distance of the Dutch East Indies. Horrified, the U.S., British, and Dutch governments cut all trading links with Japan. Negotiations dragged on through the summer and autumn, but neither Japan nor the United States would make any real concessions.

Japan's options

By October, Japan had decided to establish the Greater East Asia Co-Prosperity Sphere—in many ways a Japanese empire. The head of the Japanese government, General Hideki Tojo, announced that "the Japanese empire stands at the crossroads of its rise or fall." It was obvious that any increase in the size of the Japanese empire would clash with U.S., British, French, and Dutch interests and might threaten Australia. Given the war in Europe, the United States was the only power that could put a stop to Japan. The Japanese were only too well aware of this, and decided on a **preemptive** strike. They would destroy the U.S. Pacific Fleet, thereby taking out their main rival.

INDIE MOET VRIJ !

WERKT EN VECHT ERVOOR !

This Dutch poster shows the Greater East Asia Co-Prosperity Sphere as an octopus, reaching its tentacles out across the Dutch East Indies.

PLANNING FOR PEARL HARBOR

PLANNING FOR AN ATTACK ON THE U.S BASE AT PEARL HARBOR STARTED IN JANUARY 1941. IN NOVEMBER, THIS IS THE JAPANESE FORCE THAT SET SAIL:

6 AIRCRAFT CARRIERS	3 SUBMARINES
2 BATTLESHIPS	8 OIL TANKERS
3 CRUISERS	1 SUPPLY SHIP
9 DESTROYERS	

Pearl Harbor, December 1941

After the bombing of Pearl Harbor, the Japanese conquered more and more of Southeast Asia.

Japan lies in the West Pacific Ocean. For some years, relations between the United States and Japan had been strained. Both countries had trading interests around the Pacific Ocean. The Japanese in particular wanted to expand their trade and empire. The United States wanted to protect their trade. The U.S. eventually reacted by cutting off supplies of oil to Japan. This was a great blow to the Japanese. They had little oil or raw materials of their own. They had to either give in to U.S. pressure or fight. They decided to fight.

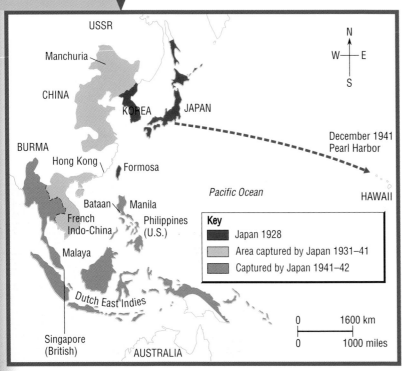

A silent approach

On November 26, 1941, the Japanese secretly set sail for Pearl Harbor. They sailed 275 miles (444 km) north of Oahu, further north than usual of the shipping lanes, so they would not meet other ships. On the night of December 6, they silently closed in on Pearl Harbor.

It was a beautiful Saturday night. The Japanese sailors tuned their radios to the U.S. stations and listened to dance band music while they waited.

There were 92 U.S. ships in Pearl Harbor, including eight big battleships. This was unusual. Normally half of the battleships were out on patrol, but because they were slow and easily bombed by airplanes, the U.S. navy was nervous. They knew the Japanese were thinking of war, so the battleships were only allowed out with aircraft carriers to escort them. It just so happened that two aircraft carriers were out ferrying airplanes to other islands in the Pacific Ocean, so the battleships stayed in.

Taken by surprise

On the morning of December 7, a Japanese submarine sneaked into Pearl Harbor. It was blown up, but where had it come from and why? Then at 7:02 A.M., two **radar** operators saw a blip on the radar screen that meant many airplanes approaching fast. They phoned headquarters and were told not to worry. Some U.S. planes were due to arrive. It must be them. The radar operators went off to breakfast.

At 7:55 A.M., Mitsuo Fuchida led the Japanese planes in to bomb Pearl Harbor. The United States could not believe it was happening. There were shattering roars and billowing clouds of smoke as torpedoes slammed into ships. Sailors tumbled from their bunks and ran to the guns as ships caught fire and started to sink. Then the Japanese pilots turned their attention to the seven airfields. The U.S. planes were all parked wing to wing because this made them easier to guard. Most of the planes were destroyed or damaged. Later in the war, planes were always dispersed around the airfield so that they would not be such a sitting target.

By 10:00 A.M., the bombing was over. The best of the U.S. battleships had been sunk or badly damaged; thousands of Americans had been wounded or killed. The Japanese flew back to their aircraft carriers while the dazed United States started to clear up.

DESTRUCTION AT PEARL HARBOR
2,403 KILLED
18 SHIPS, INCLUDING 8 MAJOR BATTLESHIPS, DESTROYED OR SERIOUSLY DAMAGED
247 AIRCRAFT DESTROYED ON THE GROUND
29 JAPANESE CARRIER CREW MEMBERS KILLED
5 JAPANESE MIDGET SUBMARINES SUNK
1 U-BOAT SUBMARINE SUNK

A triumph for Japan?

So what were the results of this one-sided battle? The Japanese were triumphant. They went on to take island after island in the Pacific Ocean for several months, while it took the United States months to recover. However, the bombing of Pearl Harbor brought the United States into the war on the Allied side, alongside Britain, against Japan and Germany. From now on, the war became truly a world war, fought all over the globe. Moreover, the U.S. aircraft carriers had escaped. They lived to fight another day and to change the way in which sea battles were fought.

This photograph shows the USS Shaw under attack during the raid on Pearl Harbor.

17

Defeat in the Far East, 1942

The Japanese invasion of Malaya

Immediately after their triumph at Pearl Harbor, the Japanese invaded the British **colony** of Malaya on December 8, 1941. The British were fighting for their survival in Europe. They had few troops in Malaya, far fewer airplanes than the Japanese, and they underestimated Japanese fighting capacities. A British battleship, the *Prince of Wales,* and the battle cruiser *Repulse* had been sunk. The British fought hard but were overwhelmed and retreated through the jungle towards Singapore. The Japanese soldiers were better jungle fighters and they also used bicycles and tanks to speed up their advance along the jungle tracks. By January 31, the British had retreated to Singapore at the tip of Malaya.

The invasion of Singapore

Singapore is a diamond-shaped island, 26 miles (42 km) long and 14 miles (22 km) wide, at the foot of the Malaya **peninsula.** In 1941, it had a busy port. There were guns defending the port but these faced the sea. The British had expected to hold Malaya so they had not expected to defend Singapore from the north. There were about 80,000 soldiers on the island, including Australian, Malay, Indian, and British troops. As the Japanese got nearer, they began bombing the island. By the beginning of February, they were close to Singapore itself. They landed a total of three divisions of soldiers. Soon they captured the three reservoirs on the island. The British surrendered and thousands of soldiers became prisoners of war without ever having fired a shot. Singapore was surrendered to the Japanese on February 15, 1942. Defeats like this weakened the British empire, and after the war it began to break up.

This Photograph shows British General Percival surrendering the British flag to the Japanese at Singapore.

The Japanese invasion of the Philippines

The U.S. commander, Lt. General Douglas MacArthur had said that he could prevent a Japanese invasion anywhere in the Philippines. However, on December 8, within ten hours of devastating the U.S. Pacific Fleet at Pearl Harbor, the Japanese began landing troops throughout the Philippine Islands. They also attacked the U.S. airfields at Formosa—now Taiwan—where they destroyed 103 aircraft, ensuring air superiority for the rest of the campaign. In December, MacArthur had to abandon the capital, Manila, and was then forced to retreat to the Bataan Peninsula.

These American soldiers suffered greatly while walking on the Bataan "Death March."

The invasion of the Philippines had been so easy that the Japanese withdrew some forces to attack the nearby Dutch **East Indies**. When they fell on February 22, 1942, the Japanese troops returned to Bataan and the U.S. forces there surrendered on April 8, 1942. When President Roosevelt had ordered MacArthur to Australia in March 1942, McArthur vowed, "I shall return"–and he did in 1944.

Corregidor and surrender

The Japanese then attacked the nearby island of Corregidor in Manila Bay. In one month, they took this fortress from the United States. The Japanese terms of surrender of May 7, 1942 included the surrender of all the Philippines to them.

Bataan Death March April 10–22, 1942

More than 70,000 Americans and Filipinos were captured and forced to march 65 miles (105 km) to Camp O'Donnell. They were beaten and starved and many who fell from exhaustion were killed. Probably 7,000–10,000 died on the march and as many escaped into the surrounding jungle. After the war, the Japanese commander, General Masaharu Homma, was tried and executed for his responsibility for the Bataan Death March, although he had been more lenient than his superiors wished.

The Battle of Coral Sea, May 1942

After Pearl Harbor, the Japanese took more and more islands in the Western Pacific Ocean. Neither the United States nor Britain could stop them.

In May 1942 the Japanese planned to invade Port Moresby. As far as the **Allies** were concerned, this was dangerously close to Australia and New Zealand. Yet what could they do? The Japanese seemed to be unstoppable.

U.S. aircraft carriers, such as the USS Enterprise, had crews of up to 3,000 men, including sailors, airmen, mechanics, cooks, and bakers.

But the United States had three advantages. First, they had three aircraft carriers in the Western Pacific. Two were the carriers that had been saved because they were out delivering airplanes when the Japanese bombed Pearl Harbor. Also, the United States had broken the Japanese codes before the war, so they could decipher many of their enemy's naval messages. By mid-April 1942, the United States knew that the Japanese were planning to invade Port Moresby with plans on bombing Australia from there. Third, the Japanese had severely damaged the U.S. battleship fleet at Pearl Harbor. So the United States was forced to adopt a new type of warfare: using aircraft carriers and airplanes instead of battleships.

The battle

By early May, the combined United States and Australian fleet was in the Coral Sea near Australia. The Japanese fleet was also. Despite rain and bad weather, both sides sent planes out and had a good idea of where each other's ships were. On May 8, the battle reached a crisis. The Allies had two aircraft carriers while the Japanese had three; but both sides had about the same number of planes and smaller ships. At dawn, despite heavy rain, both sides sent out planes that bombed and torpedoed the enemy's ships.

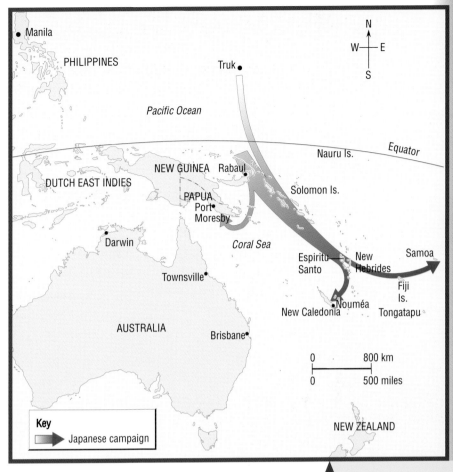

This map shows how close the Battle of Coral Sea was to Australia.

By afternoon, the U.S. carrier *Lexington* had fires raging out of control that forced the crew to abandon ship. The other U.S. carrier, *Yorktown*, was damaged. On the Japanese side, one carrier was sunk, one was destroyed, and the third had heavy losses to its air group. So the battle was a draw, but two things made it very important. It stopped Japan from invading Port Moresby and threatening Australia. It was also the first sea battle in history when the opposing sides' ships never were in sight of each other.

The plane that sank the *Lexington:*

The Nakajima B5N2 '"Kate." This was the Japanese plane in the forefront of the Pearl Harbor attack and later was involved in the sinking of the *Lexington, Yorktown,* and *Hornet.* Maximum speed: 236 mph (380 kph) at 11,811 ft (3,600 m). Maximum range: 1,234 miles (1990 km). Armament: 1, 7.7 mm machine-gun plus 1,764 lbs (800 kg) of bombs or torpedoes.

The Battle of Midway, June 1942

Admiral Isoroku Yamamoto was commander-in-chief of the Japanese Combined Fleet. He never wanted war with the United States. He was worried about Japan's ability to fight the United States in a long war. Having lived and worked in the United States, Yamamoto knew it was a rich, powerful country with enormous industries. He knew that in a year or so, the United States could have its factories making so many ships, guns, and airplanes that Japan might be overwhelmed. Therefore, the Japanese had to completely destroy the U.S. Pacific Fleet as soon as possible. Only then could they hope to dominate the Pacific Ocean and perhaps come to a peaceful agreement with the United States.

This crew on board a U.S. Navy aircraft carrier is preparing for a raid.

So Yamamoto planned the destruction of the U.S. fleet at Midway Island. Midway was in fact two tiny islands almost surrounded by a coral reef. There was a harbor and an airfield.

The plan

Yamamoto made a complicated plan. Part of the Japanese navy would invade the Aleutian Islands far to the north. While the United States rushed north to retake the Aleutians, another Japanese force would take Midway. The U.S. fleet would rush back to Midway and then the Japanese fleet would blast it from the water.

However, the United States could read the Japanese codes. They knew their enemy's plan so they sailed their fleet to Midway and waited.

The beginning of the battle

The area of the Pacific Ocean near Midway always has a lot of fog and rain in May and June, so it was difficult for planes to spot ships down below. The Japanese were not expecting the U.S. fleet so they concentrated on attacking the island of Midway. They were shocked when at 7:30 A.M. a plane reported seeing about ten U.S. ships. The battle was on and it raged all day as airplanes attacked ships on each side.

By 5 P.M., the U.S. carrier *Yorktown* was finally sunk. But this was the only carrier the United States lost, whereas the Japanese lost four aircraft carriers and twice as many airplanes. As night fell, both sides drew away from each other. This time the United States had undoubtedly won. The Battle of Midway was one of the most important battles of the War in the Pacific and a key turning point. Yamamoto knew that the Japanese could not make more and more aircraft carriers, whereas the United States was now geared up for war and could easily replace their losses. From this time on, the Japanese never won a major battle and the United States, despite some setbacks, never lost, as they moved slowly across the Pacific Ocean toward Japan.

During the Battle of Midway, a Japanese torpedo scored a direct hit on the U.S. aircraft carrier USS Yorktown.

USS *Enterprise*
One of the three U.S. aircraft carriers at Midway was the USS *Enterprise*. Planes from it and the USS *Yorktown* sank the four prized Japanese aircraft carriers. The *Enterprise* fought in every major battle in the South Pacific except the Battle of Coral Sea.

Hitler and Stalin

Japan could concentrate on the war in the Pacific without fear of attack by the Soviet Union. From June 1941, the Soviet Union was at war with Germany in a struggle that lasted for four years. Only after May 1945 did the Soviets turn eastward and join with the Allied forces against Japan.

The Soviet-German nonaggression pact, August 1939

Before World War II started, Hitler and Stalin had signed a nonaggression pact. This agreement shook the rest of the world. Hitler was fanatically anti-**communist**, yet he was signing an agreement with Stalin, the leader of the communist Soviet Union. The reason for their pact was that Hitler wanted to invade Poland without warlike objections from the Soviet Union. Stalin, for his part, knew that Hitler had no love for the Soviet Union and would attack if, and when, it suited him. The nonaggression pact bought time for the Soviet Union to move more factories to the east, beyond the Ural Mountains and beyond the reach of a German **Blitzkreig** attack; time to produce more war goods and recruit and train more soldiers. It also gave them an excuse to occupy half of Poland and the Baltic states of Lithuania, Latvia, and Estonia.

This map details Operation Barbarossa—the German attack on the Soviet Union, 1941–42.

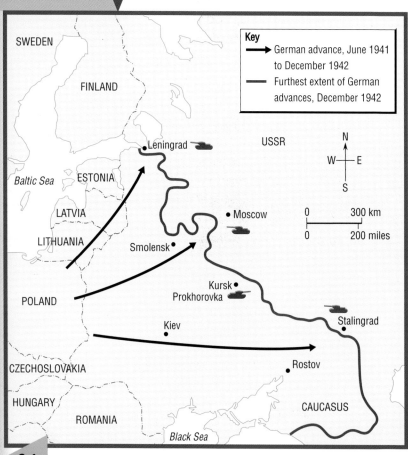

Key
→ German advance, June 1941 to December 1942
— Furthest extent of German advances, December 1942

SWEDEN

FINLAND

Leningrad

USSR

Baltic Sea

ESTONIA

LATVIA

Moscow

0   300 km
0   200 miles

LITHUANIA

Smolensk

Kursk
Prokhorovka

POLAND

Kiev

Stalingrad

CZECHOSLOVAKIA

Rostov

HUNGARY

CAUCASUS

ROMANIA

Black Sea

From Russia to the Soviet Union

Although Russia was a large country, it had suffered enormous upheavals since 1900. First, it had tried to catch up with the industrialized countries. Then it had been beset by World War I and the **Bolshevik** Revolution, which had overthrown the **czar** and set up a communist government. In 1922, it became the Soviet Union. Several years of civil war were followed by many more years of disruption, as farms and factories changed to being run by the communist government.

All this and Joseph Stalin's harsh leadership and the loss of millions of lives, had taken its toll on the country.

Operation Barbarossa, June 22, 1941

The nonaggression pact bought Stalin just over eighteen months. By the end of 1940, German advances in the west were halted by the Battle of Britain. Hitler turned east. On June 22, 1941, he invaded the Soviet Union in an attack codenamed Operation Barbarossa. Hitler's desire for **Lebensraum** for the German people was to be satisfied by taking land from Russia. However, by this time, Hitler seemed to be behaving like the French Emperor Napoleon. In 1812, Napoleon had felt himself so powerful that he could take on Russia, and he set out for Moscow with a huge army. Like Napoleon, Hitler's army advanced rapidly at first, driving deep into the Soviet Union. Could this success last?

The German army attacked with 148 divisions with more than 3 million soldiers. They inflicted massive defeats on the Soviet Army in its advance of 1941.

Britain or the Soviet Union?

Hitler did order preparations to be made for an invasion of England, but he was always half-hearted in his desire to launch a large seaborne landing. Germany, unlike Britain, was not a sea power . . . . And there was another ideological reason why Hitler was not fully committed to invading Britain. For him, it would have been a distraction. Britain contained neither the space, nor the raw materials, that he believed the new German Empire needed. And he admired the British . . . . If the Germans let themselves be drawn into a risky amphibious operation against a country Hitler had never wanted as an enemy, every day the potential threat from his greatest ideological opponent would be growing stronger . . . . All this meant that, from Hitler's point of view, there was an alternative to invading Britain: he could invade the Soviet Union.

from *War of the Century* by Laurence Rees, BBC 1999

Moscow, June 1941–March 1942

At 3:15 A.M. on June 22, 1941, a huge German army launched Operation Barbarossa. Armies of more than three million men on either side faced each other on the German-Soviet frontiers. The area over which they might be fighting was the size of half of Europe.

The Germans knew that they had to strike quickly. They had to defeat the Soviet Union before its soldiers could retreat into the vast Russian lands to the east; and they had to do it before the onset of the brutal Soviet winter. There were three main thrusts. One was in the north toward Leningrad. One was in the center toward Moscow, the capital of the Soviet Union, and the third was in the south toward the Ukraine.

These German soldiers are on the move as they advance deep into the Soviet Union.

Invasion

German armored divisions drove forward, covering at least 19 miles (30 km) a day. In the first weeks of the war, they encircled the Russian armies and took hundreds of thousands of prisoners. By July 17, the German army was 310–496 miles (500–800 km) inside Russia. However, the armored divisions were outrunning their supplies, and the infantry soldiers behind them could not keep up. Instead of capturing Moscow quickly, the armored divisions had to wait, sometimes for weeks, for ammunition, fuel, and other supplies.

The beginning of winter, 1941–1942

By October 30, the German advance had come to a halt about 62 miles (100 km) west of Moscow. The Russian soldiers had been forced to retreat, but now they were fighting harder, helped by the wet autumn weather that bogged down the German tanks and trucks. Then, as winter came, the roads started to freeze over and the Germans could move again. However, now the German soldiers did not have thick enough clothing for the severe Russian winter. Even to go outside without thick gloves on could mean frostbite in a few minutes. Moreover, the Germans found that the oil froze in their trucks, guns, and other machinery. Both these things helped the Russians in the desperate defense of their capital city.

The Soviet plan

Stalin, the Soviet leader, was a ruthless dictator. Before the war he had been worried that some of the army generals might become too powerful, so he had had many of them killed. The Germans knew this and they assumed that there were no experienced Russian generals left. The Germans were confident they could defeat such a poor army. They also thought the Russians would run out of guns, tanks, and other machinery because so many factories had been destroyed in the German invasion. However, Stalin had planned for this. He had built hundreds of factories far to the east of Moscow, beyond the Ural mountains. These factories went on producing everything from tanks to rifles, far from the invading German army. The Russians did not only move their factories, but all sorts of national treasures from museums and galleries were packed up and moved east. Also, to the surprise of the Germans, the Russian army did not collapse. It threw itself into defending the capital.

German **panzers** led the attack across the vast and empty Russian landscape.

The Battle for Moscow, 1941–1942

Three weeks before Christmas 1941, in the depths of the icy winter, the Russians counterattacked. The Germans held on, but by spring 1942, as the weather improved, there was a stalemate. Neither side was winning. This was the first time in nearly nine months that the Germans had been halted in their headlong invasion of the Soviet Union. It showed the Russians that the Germans could be stopped and that Moscow could be saved. Just as the Battle of Britain was the point at which the German forces were stopped in the West, so the Battle of Moscow was the point at which they were stopped in the East.

MEN AND TANKS AT THE BATTLE OF MOSCOW		
	SOLDIERS	TANKS
GERMAN	900,000	1,600
SOVIET	950,000	1,000

Stalingrad, August 1942–January 1943

In July 1942, Hitler decided to leave the northern and central German armies to sit tight around Leningrad and Moscow because they were in a stalemate position. The northern German army had reached the outskirts of Leningrad—now called St. Petersburg—by September 8, 1941, but they could not break the defenses. Thus began the long siege of Leningrad which lasted until 1944. Probably as many as one million Russians died in the siege, many of starvation. Around 110 tons (100 tonnes) of food a day were needed to keep the citizens of the city alive, but this was hardly ever achieved. Most people lived on one tenth of the calorie intake needed to remain healthy. The sewage system was destroyed by bombing. There was no heating and no lighting, but the people of Leningrad held on.

Supplies were brought into Leningrad across frozen Lake Ladoga.

Stalingrad

Meanwhile, Hitler planned to push south with a larger army towards Stalingrad. Stalingrad was a sprawling, industrial city on the banks of the Volga River. It was an industrial city and a communications center along the huge river as well as a key road junction. It was close to the Caucasus Mountains, an area where major Russian oil fields lay. The Germans were eager to capture the oil fields.

Stalingrad was also important for another reason. It was named after Stalin, the leader of the Soviet Union, because he had taken part in defending it during the Russian Civil War. Stalin did not want the city to fall to the Germans. He ordered that it must be held at all costs. For his part, Hitler knew that if he could take Stalingrad, it would be a crushing blow to the Russians.

By the night of August 23, the German armies had reached Rostov, and the Russians were fast running out of places in which to retreat. Stalingrad was under constant air attack. Hitler had decided to concentrate his forces on taking Stalingrad rather than the oil fields in the Caucasus. This was against the advice of his army commanders, but by this time, Hitler had fired his commander-in-chief. He assumed the position himself, and was intent on making all military decisions. The Germans encircled the city so that the only way in and out for the Russians was across the river to the east bank.

Fierce fighting

Through the late summer and early autumn, the fighting became fiercer in the city. Street by street, house by house, cellar by cellar the Germans and Russians fought for possession of the city. On September 14, the central station changed hands four times. In October, the Russians were able to bring heavier guns to fire on the Germans from the east bank. By now, the Germans knew they were running out of time. The Russian winter was approaching and the Russians were planning a counterattack.

On November 19, the Russians counterattacked. They ripped into the German defenses. In the following weeks, the Russians encircled the German 6th Army under General Friedrich Paulus. Hitler would not allow him to retreat and to encourage Paulus, he promoted him to the rank of a Field Marshal. Hitler also ordered supplies to be flown in to the trapped German army. But more than this was needed, and on January 31, 1943, Paulus and the 91,000 soldiers under his command surrendered.

Battle raged day and night in the ruined city of Stalingrad. Soviet and German soldiers fought over every house.

The cost to Germany

It is difficult to know exact figures, but the Battle of Stalingrad may have cost the Germans 1.5 million men, dead, wounded, missing, or taken prisoner. Most of these prisoners were put into Soviet labor camps. Most then died from lack of food and medicine, and being overworked. Some prisoners were not even released until ten years after the war ended. The loss of soldiers in Stalingrad was about one quarter of all the soldiers they had in Russia. It was a huge loss for Germany and an even bigger defeat. It was the beginning of the end for their campaign in Russia, and for the Russians, it was a glimmer of hope.

BATTLE FACTS

THE LIFE EXPECTANCY OF A RUSSIAN SOLDIER IN STALINGRAD WAS 24 HOURS.

OF 110,000 GERMANS TAKEN PRISONER, 5 PERCENT SURVIVED

The Battle of Kursk, July 1943

The city of Kursk lies 279 miles (450 km) south of Moscow. It is surrounded by rolling plains, rivers, and woods. In July 1943, the Germans and Russians faced each other over a long front line. Around Kursk, the front line bulged westward because the Russians had taken more land. This bulge in a front line is called a "salient." The Germans planned to cut this salient in half. They called the battle plan "Citadel."

The Germans began to assemble a huge army with many tanks and guns. The Russians knew about their plans because they could see the German buildup, but also because some of the senior German officers who were opposed to Hitler sent information to a spy ring based in Switzerland. This information was then forwarded to the Russians. Furthermore, the Russians had been building more and more tanks, aircraft, and guns in their factories in the east. They had been training more and more soldiers and had received U.S. supplies, sent from Britain by the Royal Navy to northern Russian ports. They also built trenches and put in minefields around important parts of the salient.

As well a being an effective weapon, Russian T34 tanks also transported troops into battle.

Beginning of the Battle of Kursk, July 5, 1943

In fact, the Russians did not wait for the Germans to attack. At 2 A.M. on July 5, the Russian artillery opened fire on the surprised Germans. The Battle of Kursk had begun. The German armies attacked on each side of the salient and broke through to the south. The fighting often went on all day and into the night.

By July 11, the Germans were near Prokhorovka and were closing in. The Russians were throwing in everything to stop them. On July 12, the Russian General Rotmistrov was ordered to attack. He had about 900 tanks against about the same number of German tanks. It was the biggest tank battle of World War II. But air attacks, rocket battery fire, and artillery attacks continued, too. Despite huge Russian losses, the battle turned against the Germans. At this time, Hitler heard that Americans and British forces had landed in Italy so he withdrew some of the German army from Kursk to fight in Italy. The Russians counterattacked and drove the Germans back.

Soviet women fighters

Of the twelve million front-line soldiers in the Soviet armed forces during World War II, one million were women. There were women pilots in their own air regiments, with women mechanics and ground crew. There were women tank commanders, snipers, and soldiers in addition to women working in the more traditional support roles of doctors, nurses, ambulance drivers, munitions, farm, and office workers.

Soviet supplies, tanks, and soldiers

The Germans were amazed that, however great the Russian losses, there were always fresh soldiers, more tanks, airplanes, and guns. From 1941–45, the United States and Britain provided not only food and medical supplies to Russia, but huge quantities of aircraft, tanks, trucks, and armaments.

The Germans were also surprised by the quality of the Russian tanks. These tanks were built in the east, at a huge factory in a place called Tankograd. The most popular tank was the T34. Apart from heavy armor, a powerful diesel engine, and a large gun, it had wide tracks which made it very good at crossing rough ground. The armored body was sloped rather than square, so that some shells glanced off it. But more than anything, it was reliable and easy to maintain on the battlefield.

The quality of the soldiers also surprised Germany. The soldiers were far tougher and better trained than the ones the Germans met when they first invaded the Soviet Union in 1941. By 1943, Russia was geared up for war. From this time on, the Germans never won another significant battle in Russia—or indeed, in the whole war.

*By the winter of 1943, Soviet women in the Night Bomber Regiment were flying up to fifteen combat **sorties** a night, in freezing conditions, and in open planes carrying 661 lbs. (300 kilos) of bombs.*

The Mediterranean Sea

The defeat of France in June 1940 changed the political situation around the Mediterranean Sea. Mussolini, the Italian leader and Hitler's ally, saw an opportunity to gain more land in Africa and in 1940 decided to attack British territories in North Africa.

By December, the British were fighting back. British and Australian forces took 130,000 Italian prisoners and regained control in North Africa. Victories in East Africa followed and Britain felt more sure of control of the eastern Mediterranean. However, this confidence was soon shaken when in April 1941, Germany reinforced and replaced Italy in the fighting in southeast Europe. By mid-1941, Germany had control of all of southeast Europe around the Mediterranean.

Beginning in 1943, the Allies began the assualt on Europe, first by attacking from Africa in the south, the Soviet Union in the east, and Britain in the west.

The importance of the Mediterranean Sea

The Mediterranean was vital to both sides. Loss of the use of the Mediterranean would cut off Britain from the oil fields of the Middle East and contact with India. In addition, at some future date, Britain might be able to invade German-dominated Europe from North Africa.

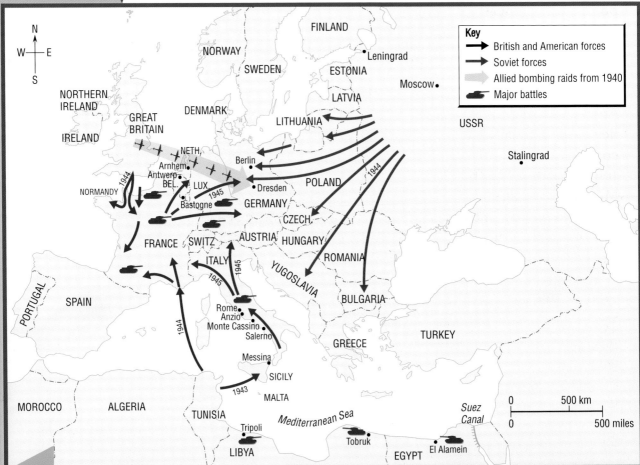

Key
- British and American forces
- Soviet forces
- Allied bombing raids from 1940
- Major battles

Rommel in North Africa

With this in view, Hitler sent General Erwin Rommel to North Africa in the spring of 1941. He was a gifted strategist and a great leader. He was soon driving the British back through Libya towards Egypt, despite reinforcements of Indian, Australian, New Zealand, and South African soldiers. By April 11, the Australian 9th Division was surrounded by Rommel at Tobruk, Libya.

These German prisoners were captured by the Allies during their conquest of Tunisia in North Africa, in 1943.

Meanwhile, Britain was more successful in the Middle East. Communications with the Soviet Union were maintained and Britain's supply routes to the oil fields and via the Gulf to India and the east were secured. Confidence in support from these areas was shaken, however, when Japan entered the war and devastated the British position in Southeast Asia.

The entry of Japan into the war in December 1941 meant that many British Commonwealth soldiers went to fight on that front rather than in North Africa. Thus, although the British forces, renamed the Eighth Army, chased Rommel 310 miles (500 km) back to Tripoli, they did not defeat him. In early summer 1942, Rommel obtained more supplies and counterattacked. This time the British were driven back to Egypt, losing Tobruk on the way. The Germans were triumphant. The British base at Malta was almost put out of action, and German **U–boats** and aircraft severely damaged British **convoys** in the Mediterranean Sea in August 1942. However, the British held on under their new commander, General Bernard Montgomery, and Rommel got no further.

Tanks in the desert

Both the Germans and British understood that tanks and guns were the dominant weapons in the open, sandy deserts of North Africa. The British used their own Crusader tanks and U.S. Stuart tanks, but the light armor of both was inferior to the heavy German tank armor. This meant that the Germans won more tank-versus-tank battles.

El Alamein, October 24–November 4, 1942

On June 22, 1942, Hitler promoted Rommel to Field Marshal. Now opposing him in North Africa was the British General Montgomery in command of the Eighth Army. Montgomery's first order was that the Eighth Army would not retreat any farther. It would hold the line at Alam Halfa. The line was about 40 miles (65 km) long, running from the sea to the Qattara Depression. This line was weakest in the south. However, despite an attack by Rommel in August, the line held and Montgomery carried on reorganizing his army. He refused to be pressed by the British government or anyone else to attack Rommel until he was sure he had the means to defeat him.

Field Marshal Erwin Rommel, on the left, led the German campaign in North Africa.

He was also helped by the **"Enigma"** code-breaker, which told the British exactly where Rommel's supply ships were. Sixty percent of German shipping was sunk before it reached North Africa.

During September and October, reinforcements arrived including 300 U.S. Sherman tanks. By October 23, Montgomery was ready. He had 230,000 men and 1,030 tanks against Rommel's 100,000 men and 500 tanks. The British also had air superiority.

The battle: October 23–November 4, 1942

The British started fighting at night with an attack from their heavy guns. Then the soldiers attacked. The fighting was fierce as the Germans threw in their tanks to stop the British attack. Rommel, who had been on sick leave in Italy, flew back to take command on October 25. Much of the fighting took place along the coast where both sides had their supply lines. One hard-fought battle was for control of Kidney Hill, which the British gained. They then used heavy artillery before launching into a tank battle with the Germans. After the battle, the Germans had only 35 working tanks left and Rommel decided to withdraw.

Hitler ordered him to stay where he was but this was futile as the British broke through the German lines on November 4 and started to sweep west. Rommel ordered a full retreat towards Tobruk.

The pursuit

Montgomery stopped to reorganize his army and then set off after the Germans. He hoped to encircle them on the coast and force them to surrender; but Rommel did not intend to be trapped like that and with the help of bad weather retreated along the coast. Montgomery realized it would be a long chase. For the next three months, the British pursued the Germans for 1,395 miles (2,250 km) along the coast of North Africa. The going was often slow, as booby traps and an increasing number of German prisoners slowed up the British.

Rommel reached the border of Tunisia on February 4, 1943. Although Montgomery had not defeated Rommel, he had pushed the Germans back. The Eighth Army had suffered 13,500 casualties in the Battle of El Alamein and Rommel had lost nearly all his tanks. The Germans, with the Italians, held out in Tunisia until May 1943 when they were decisively defeated by British and U.S. forces. By this time, Rommel himself had been disabled so he did not see the surrender of 125,000 German and nearly as many Italian soldiers to the **Allies**.

With North Africa clear, the way was open for the United States and Britain to invade Italy.

British General Montgomery often watched his troops in action from the turret of his tank during the North African campaign.

BATTLE FACTS:
BATTLE OF EL ALAMEIN OCTOBER 23–NOVEMBER 4, 1942

SEPT/OCT	ROMMEL ORDERS 500,000 MINES TO BE LAID
OCT 23/24	ARTILLERY AND AIR BOMBARDMENT
OCT 24	BRITISH ADVANCE HELD UP BY MINEFIELDS
OCT 31	BRITISH CUT THE COAST ROAD
NOV 2	FIERCE FIGHTING FOR KIDNEY HILL
NOV 3	HITLER COUNTERMANDS ROMMEL'S ORDER TO WITHDRAW
NOV 4	BRITISH BREAK THROUGH ROMMEL'S LINES

Italy and the Far East

Early in 1943, the Germans and Italians were forced out of North Africa. The British and Americans turned their attention to Italy.

On July 10, the **Allies** landed in Sicily, and by August 17, they had fought their way across the island to Messina. After this they faced the problems of landing on the mainland of Italy. Mussolini, the Italian leader, was forcibly deposed and the new Italian government considered making peace with the Allies. However, the Germans decided to reinforce Italy so that when the Allies landed they met fierce resistance.

The challenge of Italy

The Italian **peninsula** is long, narrow, and mountainous and rivers run across it. Not only does an invading army have to fight through mountains, but they have to cross large rivers. Both types of terrain are easy to defend.

The United States wanted to concentrate on northwest Europe, where the plan was to land a huge force of soldiers that would fight its way to Germany and then defeat Hitler. What they did not want was a long, drawn-out battle in Italy, which would take away manpower and weapons from France. The British argued that Italy was the "soft underbelly" of Europe and was an easier way to reach Germany than to cross heavily defended France. The United States agreed to carry on.

It took only five months of modern warfare to reduce the 1,414-year-old Monte Cassino to ruins.

Monte Cassino

The Allies fought their way to Naples and undertook landings along the coast at Salerno and Anzio. They took Naples on October 1. The mountains, the winter weather, and torrential rain held up the Allies and gave the Germans time to build defenses. Field Marshal Albert Kesselring was in charge of German defenses. He decided to stop the Allies just south of Rome at the Garigliano Valley. The line the Germans held was called the Gustav Line. Mountains rose above the valley to the north. At the western end, the Liri River cut a path, providing a route to Rome. On the corner, overlooking both valleys and dominating the route north to Rome, sat the monastery fortress of Monte Cassino. The Allies decided they must take it.

The battle began in January 1944 and by February, Allied soldiers were within 437 yards (400 m) of the monastery, but they could get no farther and suffered heavy losses. Down to a quarter of their strength, they were relieved by soldiers from India. A plan of bombing began, followed by an attack from the New Zealand Corps. More attacks followed, but despite heavy casualties, the Germans on Monte Cassino held out. The final battle for the monastery started on May 11. On May 18, Polish soldiers took the now empty shell of Monte Cassino. The Gustav Line was broken. U.S. forces took Rome on June 4, 1944.

The Allies fight on

Fighting continued in Italy until well into 1945. This meant the Germans had to keep soldiers—25 divisions—fighting there which they could have used elsewhere. It also gave the Allies much experience in landing large numbers of soldiers, tanks, and weapons from the sea onto well-defended beaches. This prepared them for D-Day.

The Far East

After Japan closed the Burma Road, U.S. aircraft flew millions of tons of supplies over the "HUMP" to U.S., Commonwealth, and Chinese forces. This kept them supplied with the minimum of weapons and food. By 1944 the **Allies** were ready to invade German-held western Europe.

The "jeep" was one of the most valuable vehicles in the war. It could drive over and through rocky hills, marshy swamps, and shifting sands. Designed for messenger service, the jeep was soon used on every front from Russia to Italy. Originally called the "General Purpose" vehicle, U.S. soldiers shortened that to GP—or "jeep"!

Merrill's Marauders

Organized in 1943, Merrill's Marauders were a group of 3,000 U.S. infantrymen fighting under the command of General Frank Merrill. Volunteering to take part in "dangerous and hazardous" missions, Merrill and his soldiers helped develop a style of tough jungle combat that constantly wrecked havoc on Japanese soldiers, supply lines, and communications.

The Beaches of Normandy, June 1944

By 1944, strategic "around the clock bombing" by the RAF and the U.S. Army Air Corps weakened German industry, making an Allied invasion of mainland Europe possible. Allied leaders hoped that tactical bombing would slow German reactions to any invasion.

Operation Overlord

U.S. General Dwight D. Eisenhower was chosen as the Supreme Allied Commander of the invasion. The invasion was code-named "Overlord," and it was planned for June 1944 when the weather should be fairly good. It was very important that the place at which the Allies would land was kept secret. The obvious place to cross the English Channel was at the narrowest part, across the Straits of Dover, and this was where the Germans had most of their troops. In fact, the Allies chose Normandy.

These U.S. soldiers are landing on Omaha Beach on D-Day, June 6, 1944.

The Allies used about 7,000 ships, of which 4,000 carried soldiers and weapons to land on the beaches. The other 3,000 were either to bombard the Germans from the sea or to carry supplies. The Allies also needed harbors. Since large ships could not sail close to the beaches, huge artificial harbors, known as "Mulberries," were built. These were then towed across the Channel to Normandy. An ingenious underwater oil pipe was also built, code-named Pluto.

D-Day 1944

On June 6, 1944, the Allied invasion began. The weather was bad. Hundreds of soldiers felt seasick as they headed for Normandy. Each soldier had enough food to last him for 24 hours, French money, and his pack. Thousands of ships sailed through the night protected by thousands of airplanes. The best-planned invasion ever was under way. It was like moving a large floating city to France in one day.

The beaches were defended with mines, barbed wire, and wooden obstacles in the water. Major General Hobart of the British 79th Armored Division thought up different ways of getting through the German defenses, including minesweeping tanks and bridge-laying tanks.

The landings were made on five beaches, which had code names. Sword, Juno, and Gold were British and Canadian beaches. Omaha and Utah were U.S. beaches. During the night, paratroopers and gliders had been dropped to attack German guns. By early morning, the Allied ships were coming up to the beaches. Soldiers rushed ashore while the large ships bombarded the German guns. The Americans had a difficult landing on Omaha. There were cliffs defended by the best German troops along the coast. However, after losses of about 3,000 soldiers, Omaha beach was taken.

By the end of the first day, the Allies had landed 156,000 men on the five beaches and they were not going to be pushed back into the sea. The next day, the Mulberry harbors were put in place and then the big ships could tie up and unload their cargoes of tanks and trucks to support the invading army. One of the Mulberries was immediately destroyed by a storm, but the other one remained intact.

General Eisenhower talked to American paratroopers of the 101st Airborne Division as they prepared for the invasion of France.

Onwards to Germany

D–Day was just the first day of the invasion. It took weeks of bitter fighting to push the Germans back. Day after day, more soldiers were landed on the Normandy beaches until the Allies captured ports and could use real harbors to land men and supplies. By August, the Allies had fought their way to Paris. By September, they hoped to cross the Rhine.

D–Day was vitally important. If the Germans had pushed the Allied soldiers off the beaches on June 6, the course of the war would have changed dramatically. It is unlikely that the Germans could have won, but the Russians could have made peace on their own terms without consulting the Americans and British.

FORCES AVAILABLE ON D-DAY	GERMAN	ALLIES
FRONT-LINE FORCES	580,000	156,000
RESERVES	850,000	2,000,000

THE ALLIES HAD KEPT THE SECRET OF WHERE THEY WOULD LAND SO WELL THAT THE GERMANS COULD NOT CONCENTRATE ALL THEIR FRONT-LINE FORCES IN TIME TO DRIVE THE ALLIES BACK INTO THE SEA.

Battle of the Bulge, Dec. 1944–Jan. 1945

Following the landings in Normandy, the **Allies** then had to fight their way to Germany. It was not easy. Hitler knew the Allies needed enormous amounts of supplies for their armies. All these had to come from bases in Britain across the English Channel. Therefore, Hitler ordered that all the French Channel ports must be held. So Le Havre, Boulogne, Calais, and Dunkirk were held like fortresses. This meant that however far east the Allies got, they still had to truck all their supplies from Normandy. This slowed up their advance.

On September 4, the Allies took the Belgium port of Antwerp. This should have helped them because large supply ships could come into Antwerp. However, Hitler had ordered that the fortress farther out at the mouth of the river be held at all costs. So, although the Allies held Antwerp, if ships tried to sail up the river to it they would be blown up. It took the Allies until November 28 to open the river. All this time they were short of supplies, such as gas and could not drive forward. It was at this point that Hitler decided to attack.

The weather was so bad that the Allied planes could neither see nor bomb the German forces. Moreover, the Allies were not expecting the Germans to attack in the hilly part of Belgium. Also, the Germans kept radio silence, so the Allies had not been able to listen to coded German army orders and decipher what was happening.

The Germans attack

The Germans struck on December 16, 1944, to the surprise of the U.S. Army leaders. The U.S. troops fought bravely, but were overwhelmed. The Germans rushed on. American troops reacted quickly. There was fierce fighting around the village of Bastogne. Surrounded U.S. troops were asked to surrender but refused and fought on. The weather improved on December 23 and the Allies fought back with airplanes as well as soldiers. Allied ships were arriving at Antwerp with supplies.

The Germans, however, were running out of gas. They had failed to capture a key Allied gas depot.

The "Bulge"

In early January, the British and U.S. forces attacked the "bulge" created by the advancing German troops. They cut through and by January 8, the Germans were surrendering. This was the end of what became known as the Battle of the Bulge.

Two German foot soldiers pass by a burning tank during the Battle of the Bulge.

The Germans suffered more than 100,000 casualties to the Allies' 76,000. But Germany had not only lost soldiers, they had lost 600 tanks and 1,600 aircraft. At this stage of the war, they could not afford to lose so much. They delayed the Allies on their way to conquer Germany by about six weeks. However, it was obvious that this would be their last real attempt to stop the Allies from reaching Germany.

The Germans were collapsing but the fighting went on for months as the Allies fought their way into Germany. The Germans blew up bridges over rivers as they retreated so Allied engineers had to build new bridges to get their soldiers across. This took time. Meanwhile the Russians were advancing on Germany from the east. In fact, most of the German army was fighting the Russians in the east.

On April 25, 1945, the Russian and the Allied advance troops met on the Elbe River and shook hands. Meanwhile, other Russian forces had reached Berlin, and to avoid capture, Hitler committed suicide on April 30. Germany surrendered a week later, and the war in Europe was over.

GENERAL MCAULIFFE: "NUTS"

SURROUNDED BY ADVANCING GERMAN TROOPS, THE COMMANDING U.S. GENERAL IN BASTONGNE, ANTHONY MCAULIFFE, GAVE A ONE-WORD REPLY TO THE GERMAN DEMAND FOR SURRENDER: "NUTS," CONFUSING THE GERMANS BUT INSPIRING HIS OWN TROOPS.

The End: The Fight for the Pacific

After the Battle of Midway in June 1942, the United States began to work its way toward Japan. Fighting alongside Australian forces in the Southwest Pacific Ocean they eventually secured New Guinea. New Guinea lies close to Australia and it was important to hold it so the Japanese could not invade Australia.

In August 1942, U.S. forces invaded Guadalcanal in their first offensive operation. From this point on, the Allies were able to stage aircraft and ships for the "island hopping" campaign toward the heart of the Japanese Empire. The **Allies** fought for island after island. Often the fighting was very fierce because the Japanese were trained to never surrender. It took until February 1943 to clear the jungle island of Guadalcanal.

Throughout 1943, both the United States and Japan worked to strengthen their grip on the islands they held. But the advantage had tipped toward the United States. There were three main reasons for this.

These U.S. marines are proudly holding up Japanese flags captured during the battle for Iwo Jima.

The United States was now making huge numbers of new ships. In 1943 alone, they made more ships than all of Japan's navy had at the beginning of the war. Second, the Japanese were losing more planes and aircrews than they could make or train. The United States was making large numbers of planes and training more pilots. Third, although it took the United States six months to capture Guadalcanal, they eventually did it and showed that Japan could be defeated.

The fighting went on. The United States took to island hopping. Sometimes they left an island to the Japanese and went on to the next one. All the time they were heading for Japan itself. Far from getting tired of the war as the Japanese hoped, the Americans were becoming more determined that nothing less than the total defeat of Japan would do.

To Okinawa and Hiroshima

By mid-1944, the United States was planning for the invasion of Japan. But how was this to be done? Airplanes were enormously important. They were needed to protect ships carrying soldiers to invade Japan and to bomb the enemy. The United States needed air bases within reach of Japan. Both the United States and Japan knew that the islands of Iwo Jima and Okinawa were important. U.S. planes could fly from these islands to bomb Japan and to protect an invasion fleet.

First, the United States took the small volcanic island of Iwo Jima 806 miles (1,300 km) from Japan. This was important as it was the first invasion of "traditional" Japanese territory. It was also used as an emergency field for the B-29 bombers that were attacking Japan from bases in the Marianas. Then they invaded Okinawa, which is only 372 miles (600 km) from Japan. They bombarded the island from ships for several weeks. The Japanese countered this with kamikaze attacks. They filled old planes with bombs and taught young pilots to fly them. The pilots flew straight into the U.S. and British ships like human bombs—these were suicide missions.

These Australian soldiers are coming ashore from a landing craft during the Pacific campaign, where they fought closely with the American troops.

The invasion began on Easter Sunday, April 1, 1945. Japan fought hard and it took more than two months to take the whole of Okinawa. The U.S. forces could now reach Tokyo, the capital of Japan. They were getting nearer to invading Japan, but Okinawa made one other thing clear. The Japanese had lost nine men for every U.S. soldier lost. They would fight for Japan to the death. If the United States invaded Japan, it might mean the deaths of a million or more Allied soldiers. It was this fear that led the Allies to decide to use the atom bomb on Hiroshima on August 6, 1945 and on Nagasaki on August 9. Japan surrendered and the war was over.

THE COST OF OKINAWA	
JAPANESE LOSSES	110,000 SOLDIERS AND OVER 110,000 CIVILIANS DEAD
ALLIED LOSSES	50,000 DEAD AND WOUNDED

A World at War–A Map of Key Battles

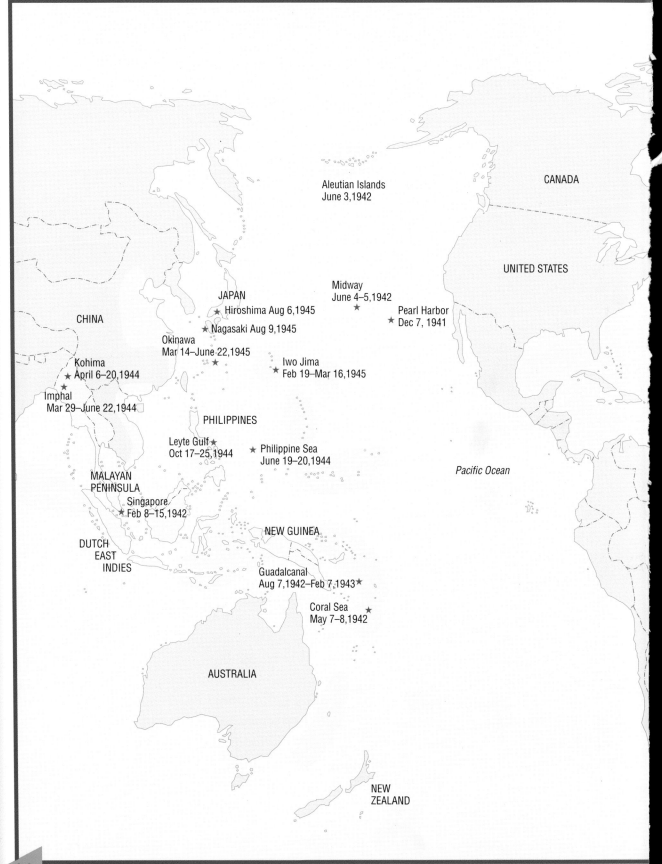

Aleutian Islands
June 3,1942

CANADA

UNITED STATES

JAPAN

★ Hiroshima Aug 6,1945

★ Nagasaki Aug 9,1945

Midway
June 4–5,1942
★

Pearl Harbor
★ Dec 7, 1941

CHINA

Okinawa
Mar 14–June 22,1945
★

Iwo Jima
★ Feb 19–Mar 16,1945

Kohima
★ April 6–20,1944

Imphal
Mar 29–June 22,1944

PHILIPPINES

Leyte Gulf ★
Oct 17–25,1944

★ Philippine Sea
June 19–20,1944

MALAYAN
PENINSULA

Singapore
★ Feb 8–15,1942

NEW GUINEA

Pacific Ocean

DUTCH
EAST
INDIES

Guadalcanal
Aug 7,1942–Feb 7,1943 ★

Coral Sea
May 7–8,1942 ★

AUSTRALIA

NEW
ZEALAND

Battle of the Atlantic
May,1939–Sept,1945

NORWAY   FINLAND   Leningrad
SWEDEN   ★ Sept 8,1941–Jan 15,1944   SOVIET UNION

BRITAIN   Bulge   Moscow
IRELAND   Dec 16,1944–Jan 28,1945 ★ Sept 30–Dec 5,1941

Dunkirk   ★ Kursk July 20,1943
May 26–June 2,1940 ★ Arnhem   ★ Stalingrad
D-Day Beaches   ★ POLAND   Aug 19,1942–Jan,1943
June 6,1944   GERMANY
FRANCE

ITALY
Anzio Jan 22–May 25,1944 ★
Monte Cassino Jan 17–May 18,1944 ★

TUNISIA   ★ Crete May 30–31,1941

ALGERIA   LIBYA   ★ El Alamein   INDIA
                        Oct 23–Nov 4,1942
Atlantic Ocean   EGYPT

AFRICA

Indian Ocean

SOUTH
AMERICA

N
W   E
S

Key
[ ] Area of conflict
★   Major battles

45

World War II Timeline

Year	Western Europe	Russian Front	Mediterranean/ North Africa	Far East
1939	Sept 1: Germany invades Poland Sept 3: Britain at war			
1940	Dunkirk, Battle of Britain			
1941		Germany invades USSR		Pearl Harbor
1942		Aug: Stalingrad Leningrad besieged	Oct–Nov: El Alamein	Feb: Singapore April: Philippines May: Coral Sea June: Midway
1943		Feb: Stalingrad July: Kursk	July 10: Allies invade Italy via Sicily	
1944	June: D-Day Dec: Battle of the Bulge	Jan: siege of Leningrad ends	May: Monte Cassino	April: Kohima May–June: Imphal
1945	May: Germany surrenders			Feb-May: Iwo Jima Mar-June: Okinawa Aug: Hiroshima Nagasaki Japan surrenders

More Books to Read

Nonfiction

Black, Wallace B., and Jean F. Blashfield. *Battle of the Bulge.* Parsippany, NJ.: Silver Burdett Press, 1993.

Humble, Richard. *A World War II Submarine.* Lincolnwood, Ill.: N T C Contemporary Publishing Company, 1991.

McGowan, Tom. *The Battle for Iwo Jima.* Danbury, Conn.: Children's Press, 1990.

Sanford, William R. *WW II Soldier at Monte Cassino.* Danbury, Conn.: Children's Press, 1991.

Stein, R. Conrad. *D-Day.* Danbury, Conn.: Children's Press, 1993.

Tames, Richard. *Pearl Harbor: The US Enters World War II.* Chicago: Heinemann Library, 1998.

Taylor, Mike. *The Great Battles of World War II.* Minneapolis: ABDO Publishing Company, 1998.

Fiction

Banks, Sara Harrell. *Under the Shadow of Wings.* New York: Simon & Schuster, 1997.

Elmer, Robert. *Into the Flames.* Minneapolis: Bethany House Publishers, 1995.

Kudlinski, Kathleen V. *Pearl Harbor is Burning!: A Story of World War II.* New York: Penguin Putnam Books for Young Readers, 1993.

Patterson, Don. *Fighter Escort.* Eden Prairie, Minn.: Hindsight, Limited, 1999.

Westall, Robert. *The Machine Gunners.* New York: William Morrow, 1997.

Glossary

Allies countries fighting against Germany and Japan, including the British, French, Soviet Union, and United States

appeasement to keep the peace by giving in to demands

Blitzkreig sudden, overwhelming attack ("lightening war" in German)

Bolsheviks political party in Russia that believed in communism. The Bolsheviks, led by Lenin, siezed power in Russia during the Russian Revolution in November 1917

chancellor chief minister, or leader

colony country that was taken over and run by another country

communist person believing in a classless society with all land and means of production owned by the state

convoy group of ships or trucks traveling together

czar emperor of Russia

Czechoslovakia country in central Europe bordering Germany to the east, which is now the Czech Republic and Slovakia

destroyer small, fast warship

East Indies group of islands in the Far East, many of which were Dutch colonies.

Enigma machine used by the Germans to make codes for their armed forces to use

evacuation moving people to a place of safety

fascist person believing in extreme nationalism and restriction on individual freedom

glider troops soldiers who parachuted from or landed with gliders

Indo-China land in the Far East, including what is now called Vietnam, Cambodia, and Laos

Lebensraum German word meaning "living space"

Luftwaffe German air force

Maginot Line line of forts built by France to stop a German attack

panzer name for a German armored vehicle, often a tank

paratrooper soldier who parachutes from an airplane

peninsula piece of land that is almost an island

preemptive attacking first to stop enemy action

propaganda spreading facts or information to help a cause

radar use of high-powered radio pulses for locating objects. Radar stands for radio detection and ranging.

reparations giving things, usually money, to repair damage of some kind

sorties missions or attacks

stock market place where stocks and shares are traded

treaty agreement between countries

Treaty of Versailles treaty the Allies made Germany sign at at the end of World War I

U-boat German submarine, short for *Unterseeboot*

Index